BIRDS
and their NESTS

Olive L. Earle

PURPLE HOUSE PRESS
KENTUCKY

INDEX

Published by Purple House Press
Classic Living Books for Kids and Young Adults
purplehousepress.com

Written and illustrated by Olive L. Earle in 1952.
Nesting areas and species information updated for 2024 with information from
the Cornell Lab of Ornithology, the National Audubon Society, and Encyclopædia Britannica.
Ruby-throated Hummingbird cover illustration by Edwin Sheppard, 1882.
Copyright © 2024 by Purple House Press. All rights reserved.
ISBN 9798888180730 paperback   ISBN 9798888180969 hardcover

How do birds know the way to build their nests? Nobody knows. By instinct the bird, perhaps building a nest for the first time, makes a nest similar in plan to the ones built by its ancestors. The typical plan is followed, even though the typical materials are sometimes replaced by others more easily found near the nesting site. Nest-building plans fall, more or less, into groups. There are nests that are open at the top and are built in trees, bushes, vines, or on the ground. There are some that have a roof and some that hang from a tree branch. There are birds that choose a hole in a tree and others that prefer a hole in the ground. Some birds make no nest at all. A nest may be built in the region that is the bird's year-round home or, in the case of a migrating bird, it may be built after a long journey. The general nesting areas given in this book are not always the entire range. Because birds do not recognize geographical boundaries, their nesting site may extend outside these areas.

A pair of BALD EAGLES uses the same nest, open to the sky, year after year. Occasionally built on an inaccessible cliff, it is more often in a high treetop. Every year the nest is repaired with fresh sticks and other coarse material until it may grow to be twenty feet deep and nine feet across. It is lined with grass and roots. From one to three rough, dull white eggs are laid; about five weeks later the downy, whitish birds are hatched. At the end of three weeks the real feathers begin to show. At first the young birds' feathers are mainly black, though white below the surface. Later the plumage is grayer, and by the end of the third year the dark-brown adult plumage and white, "bald" head and tail appear. Young birds stay in the nest for three months or more; then they are able to fly. Until the nestlings can feed themselves, their parents tear in pieces the fish or small animals they bring to the nest. Though Bald Eagles sometimes fish for themselves, they often steal fish caught by ospreys or pick up dead fish from the water's edge. Strangely enough, the young birds are, for a time, larger than their parents. The female eagle, larger than the male, may be forty-three inches long.

NESTING AREA: most of the continental U.S. and Canada. During the mid-twentieth century Bald Eagles became rare; after successful conservation efforts they were removed from the Endangered Species list in 2007.

The open nest of the GREAT HORNED OWL is usually a ready-made one, high in a tree—the deserted nest of a crow, hawk, or squirrel. Large and untidy, it is made of sticks, roots, twigs, and weed stalks. The owl repairs it and adds a few breast feathers as a lining. Sometimes the female lays her two or three nearly round white eggs in a hollow tree or on a ledge in a cave, where the nest is nothing but a few bones and bits of fur or the feathers of her victims. These fiercest of all owls swoop silently through the night, killing the birds and animals that are their food. Sometimes they catch chickens and young turkeys; but they do good, too, for they kill rabbits, rats, mice, and other crop-destroying animals. They capture their prey with their feet, which are equipped with strong, sharp claws. The legs and feet are feathered. The outer toe of each foot, like that of the ospreys, is reversible so that the bird can grasp a branch firmly, with two toes in front and two behind while tearing the meal to pieces. Indigestible parts are thrown up in the form of pellets. This great terror of the woods has a wing spread of almost five feet, and two feet or more in

6

length. The soft, fluffy feathers are grayish brown above, with black and buff markings; below, they are whitish with dark bars. The throat is clear white. The ear feathers, standing up like horns, are about two inches long. Great Horned Owls nest very early in the year. The parents share the task of sitting on the eggs. In cold areas, the sitting bird is sometimes covered with snow. The baby birds are covered with down at first. They stay in the nest for two months, and by that time their flight feathers have grown.

NESTING AREA: across North America up to the northern tree lines.

The OSPREY, or fish hawk, builds a huge open nest. Very often an old nest will be used year after year. The structure, continuously rebuilt, gets more and more bulky until the tree may break with the weight, tumbling the nest to the ground. Occasionally the birds use the fallen mass for a nursery. Ospreys like to build on the top of a dead pine or some other leafless tree. Sometimes they choose a telephone pole or a chimney. Lined with seaweed or a few feathers, the nest is made of sticks, weed stalks, and all sorts of rubbish. Usually three eggs are laid. Ospreys' eggs vary in color and markings; often they are heavily blotched. When hatched, the young birds are covered with down. Ospreys live entirely on fish, which they get by plunging into shallow water for them. In order to be near their food supply, groups of these birds nest near large rivers or along the seashore. A wriggling, slippery fish is caught in the bird's large feet, which have rough spiny scales on the soles. The fish is held head foremost. Reversible outer toes help the bird to hold the fish securely. Besides, the claws are much curved and act as pincers. Circling above their nests, these birds call with a thin, high-pitched whistle.

Ospreys are blackish-brown above and white below, and they are about twenty-four inches long.

NESTING AREA: most states and Canada, plus Ospreys are one of the few birds with worldwide distribution.

In the East, purple grackles often build their homes
in the outer walls of the Ospreys' huge nests.

The HOATZIN, of South America, builds an open nest of loosely arranged sticks. It is usually placed in the top of a small tree overhanging the edge of a forest river. Two or three whitish eggs, blotched with reddish brown, are laid. The baby birds are covered with a thin fuzz. When they are a day old, they start actively crawling around the nest. To help them scramble among the sticks, these strange nestlings use their bills as grasping hooks. Each of their wings is fitted with claws, so the young birds climb as though they had four legs. These claws disappear as the bird matures. The fossil of the oldest known bird also has claws on the wings.

If a baby Hoatzin is scared, she dives from the nest into the water below and seems able to take good care of herself there. The mother bird feeds the little ones on predigested leaves until they are old enough to pick their own. Adult Hoatzins are shades of brown marked with white, and there is yellow on the tail and the long crest feathers. Because of weak flight muscles, they do very little flying and never go far from their home area. Apparently they are protected from their enemies by their strong odor, which has earned the Hoatzin the name of "stink bird." They live in small groups.

NESTING AREA: Amazonia and the lowlands of northern South America

The MOURNING DOVE'S open nest is a flimsy, slightly hollowed platform made of a few sticks loosely thrown together. It is sometimes scantily lined with a few pieces of dried grass. These birds choose many different nesting sites, which vary from the ground to a branch fifteen feet above it. They may select a bush, a thicket, or a cactus. The two white eggs, which always seem to be in danger of falling through the untidy latticework, are hatched in about two weeks. The helpless baby birds are fed on a fluid called "pigeon milk," which is pumped up from the parents' crops. Later on, they are fed on partly digested food. Mourning Doves eat gravel to crush the hard weed seeds which they swallow whole. They also eat a few insects. Before the young birds are able to take care of themselves, the mother may lay a second batch of eggs. Mourning Doves raise three or four families a season. These cooing birds are about twelve inches long. Their general color is purplish brown or grayish blue above and pinkish buff below. The male has iridescent neck feathers.

NESTING AREA: lower 48 states, southern Canada and many parts of Mexico.

11

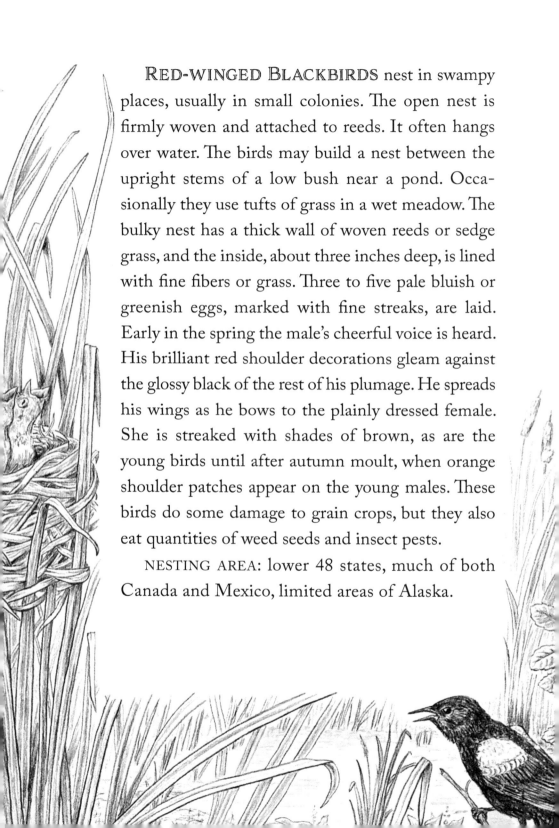

RED-WINGED BLACKBIRDS nest in swampy places, usually in small colonies. The open nest is firmly woven and attached to reeds. It often hangs over water. The birds may build a nest between the upright stems of a low bush near a pond. Occasionally they use tufts of grass in a wet meadow. The bulky nest has a thick wall of woven reeds or sedge grass, and the inside, about three inches deep, is lined with fine fibers or grass. Three to five pale bluish or greenish eggs, marked with fine streaks, are laid. Early in the spring the male's cheerful voice is heard. His brilliant red shoulder decorations gleam against the glossy black of the rest of his plumage. He spreads his wings as he bows to the plainly dressed female. She is streaked with shades of brown, as are the young birds until after autumn moult, when orange shoulder patches appear on the young males. These birds do some damage to grain crops, but they also eat quantities of weed seeds and insect pests.

NESTING AREA: lower 48 states, much of both Canada and Mexico, limited areas of Alaska.

PIED-BILLED GREBES are at home in marsh or pond. The open nest often floats like a raft on the water. Made of rotting plants brought up from the bottom, it is supported on a buoyant platform of green stems of water plants. In very shallow water, the nest is sometimes placed on broken-down reeds. It is a foot or more across. When the mother bird leaves her six to nine whitish eggs, she hides them by drawing water-soaked nesting material over them. The newly hatched birds, which are covered with down, are able to swim and dive almost as soon as they are out of their shells. Grebes do not fly readily and are awkward on land, but in the water they are extremely expert. Their peculiar toes have flaps of skin along the edges. The satiny plumage is brownish black above, lighter brown and white below. Their unusually thick bill has a black band encircling it.

NESTING AREA: lower 48 states, Mexico, much of both Canada and South America.

The YELLOW WARBLER'S open nest is fastened securely to the small branches that support it or is firmly fixed in a tree crotch. The birds like willows or elders near water, but also frequently build in the low branches of apple trees in an orchard or in shrubs or thickets in a garden. For their neatly constructed cup-shaped nests, they collect all kinds of silver-gray plant fiber. They also gather fuzz from young fern fronds, which mat into a sort of felt. Hair, plant down, and fine grass make a soft pad for the three to five eggs, which are whitish, spotted, and splashed around the larger end with dark markings. Yellow Warblers—about five inches long—are often chosen by the cowbird as foster parents for her young. The eight-inch-long Cowbird builds no nest of her own, but lays her eggs (white, spotted with brown) in the nest of various small birds. If the female

Yellow Warbler hatches the strange egg in her nest, the young cowbird is larger then her own babies. The strong cowbird gets most of the food and may even push the other nestlings out of the nest. Sometimes the Yellow Warbler wisely builds a second nest over the eggs in the first one, and lays another set of eggs. If the lazy Cowbird visits the new nest, too, the smaller birds build again over the intruder's egg. The final nursery may be the top one of the three-storied structure. The male Yellow Warbler is all yellow in general appearance: he has a yellow head and is rich olive-yellow above; below, he is bright yellow with brownish-red streaks on his breast. The female and the young birds are greener and duller in color. These useful birds destroy great numbers of insect pests.

NESTING AREA: Alaska, Canada, lower 48 states, Mexico in the Sierra Madre Occidental mountains.

The AMERICAN REDSTART'S open cup-shaped nest is built in the fork of a sapling or snug against the trunk of a small tree. The compact, well-built nest is made of thin strips of bark, dry grass, plant down, and fiber—all neatly lashed with spiders' webs. Sometimes the birds tear open withered dandelions for the sake of the immature seed "parachutes" inside, and fly off with a mouthful of soft down. The nest is lined with fine grass and hair. The four or five whitish eggs are spotted with reddish brown and lilac at the larger end. The mother bird sits on the eggs, but the father works hard helping to feed the nestlings. Redstarts are the most restless members of the active warble family. With wings and tail spread, they dart along the branches or make wild dashes up in the air or down to the ground. From twig to tree trunk they flit endlessly, looking for insects and larvae. The adult male, about five and one half inches long, is shining black above and white below, with flame-colored patches on his tail, wings, and sides. The female and young males are gray, greenish brown, and yellow. The redstart likes damp woodlands, but is also found in secluded gardens if there is water nearby. NESTING AREA: Eastern states and diagonally to the Northwest, much of Canada.

The open nest of the RUBY-THROATED HUMMINGBIRD is an exquisite nursery. It is very small and so well camouflaged with lichen and moss that it looks like part of the branch to which it is fastened with spiders' webs. In the nest, which is about three quarters of an inch across the inside, two tiny white eggs are typically laid, although there may be one or three. The nest stretches to fit the growing babies. NESTING AREA: east of the Rockies, lower portions of Canada.

The open nest of the ROSE-BREASTED GROSBEAK is a shallow saucer-shaped collection of wiry roots, twigs, and grasses. It rests insecurely on a slender branch, in a tree fork, or in vines. The nest may tip in the wind and spill out the eggs. The three to five eggs are greenish blue, blotched with brownish spots. These birds, about eight and one half inches long, belong to the finch family. NESTING AREA: Eastern states, west to the plains, southern and parts of western Canada.

The CHIPPING SPARROW builds a rather shallow open nest. Though it looks loosely made, it is skillfully woven of fine curly rootlets and fine grass. It is always lined with hair, preferably horsehair. Sometimes, if the birds can find enough of it, they build the entire nest of hair from horses, human beings, cows, or deer. This habit has earned this sparrow one of its nicknames, hair bird. Their only song is a rapidly repeated "chip!" all on one note, which is why they are called Chipping Sparrows. These birds, which are very tame and sociable, like to build their nest close to a house, well hidden in a vine, bush, or evergreen tree. They seldom build their nest more than five feet from the ground, and sometimes choose the low branch of an apple tree. Between two and seven eggs are laid; they are bluish green with a few fine spots of blackish brown and dark scrawls at the larger end. The young birds are fed chiefly on caterpillars. Chipping Sparrows are great insect eaters; they also eat some weed seeds, especially when the caterpillar season is over. They usually feed on the ground. The grown birds are about five and one half inches long. Like all other sparrows, chippies are members of the finch family, but they can be easily distinguished from their relatives. The chippy is identified by a black bill, a reddish-brown cap, a broad white or very pale gray stripe over the eye, and a dark stripe right across the eye. The tail is deeply forked. The male and female look alike. The young birds do not wear a cap, are more reddish above and more buff below, and have dark broken streaks on the breast. The Western Chipping Sparrow is larger but paler than the Eastern variety.

NESTING AREA: most of the lower 48 states and Canada, southern Alaska, parts of Mexico along the Sierra Madre mountain range.

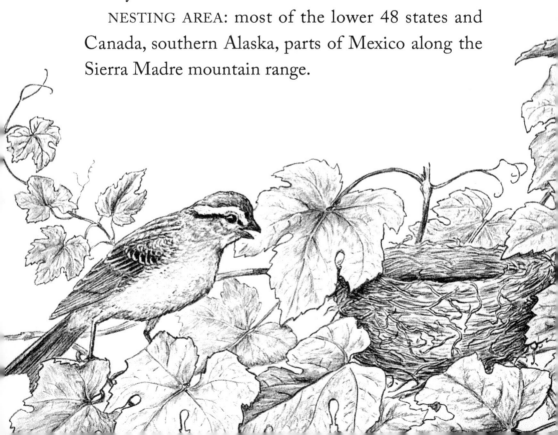

The BOBOLINK builds an open nest, but it is often almost entirely roofed over by the tall meadow grass that surrounds it. The place chosen for the nest is a depression in the ground at the base of a tuft of grass. Made of coarse grass, weed stems, and sometimes a few leaves, the shallow bowl is lined with fine grass. The nest is completely hidden by the tall grasses, but the mother bird does not rely on that alone to keep it secret. When she leaves the nest, she does not take to the air at once. Instead, she runs through the grass for some distance before she starts to fly. In the nest there may be from four to six eggs, or rarely seven. Bobolink eggs vary in color from white to shades of gray or reddish brown with irregular markings of browns and purples. The male bird guards the nest and gives a warning call when he expects danger. He spends much of his time calling his name, "Bobolink!" and singing his wild, varied song, often filling the air with rich

melody as he flies. The adult birds are about seven inches long. In the spring and early summer the male has black and white upper parts and is shiny black below, his pointed tail feathers are black, and there is a large patch of light buff at the back of his head. Before the end of the summer he loses his plumage, and his new feathers have much the same quiet coloring as the female's. She is buff-brown with dark stripes on the upper parts. The young birds, which look like their mother, are fed on insects at first. Later they learn to eat weed and grass seed. Bobolinks are useful in the areas where they nest, for there they destroy many insect pests. But when large flocks of the birds are migrating they feast off valuable crops. Coming north in the spring, they eat sprouting shoots, and in the autum, as the flocks fly south (where they are called rice birds or reed birds), they get fat on the ripening rice.

NESTING AREA: Eastern states and diagonally northwest, including portions of southern Canada.

AMERICAN WHITE PELICANS build their open nests on the ground, usually on the shore of a secluded island in an inland lake. They scrape up a mound of sandy soil some six inches high, and cover it with sticks and weeds. Sometimes the entire nest is built of matted reeds. Pelicans live in great colonies, with their nests very close together. Each nest is the home of one or two young birds. When they hatch from the white eggs, which have a chalky crust, the baby pelicans are helpless, blind, and naked. Soon they become active and are covered with thick down. By the end of three months the young birds have regular feathers. These are white, except for some gray on the head and black on the wings. The pouch, hanging from the lower bill, is yellow. The youngsters have fish soup many times each day. It consists of fish digested by the parent birds, and to get it, the little ones push their heads into their mother's or father's pouch. Later, the young birds learn to swim after their own food. American White Pelicans use the pouches on their bills as dip nets to scoop up fish. Fully grown birds have bills at least twelve inches long. The adults weigh up to twenty pounds. They are about five feet long and may be nine feet across their wings. Pelicans are

clumsy on the ground and some have difficulty rising from it, but once in the air they fly with ease. With heads drawn back and feet outstretched, these birds alternate flapping their black-tipped wings with sailing through the air. They are very much at home in the water, where they feed on surface fish. Sometimes a group of pelicans form a semicircle and, with much splashing, drive the fish before them until they have collected a fish feast that can be scooped up. Pelicans have peculiar webbed feet. Many water birds have three front toes connected by a membrane, with the hind toe left free, but the pelican's fourth toe is connected by a web to the front toes. Male and female pelicans have similar plumage. In the nesting season a horny knob appears on their upper bills; this temporary adornment soon falls off.

NESTING AREA: areas of the northern plains states and Canada, a few locations along the Texas coast and Mexico.

Large colonies of AMERICAN FLAMINGOS build their open nests on the ground at the edge of a marsh or swamp. The nests are compact mounds of mud scraped up by the birds. Built high enough to prevent their being flooded, they may be only a few inches high or over a foot, depending on the possible rise of the water. Each mound is shaped like a cone with the point cut off and measures about twelve inches across the top and about eighteen across the base. The top is hollowed to form a shallow cup, so that the single egg cannot roll off. This nest is left unlined. The white, chalky egg has a shell so thick that it takes a chick twenty-four hours to peck its way out. When the mother bird is sitting on the nest with her long red legs doubled under her, she busies herself preening feathers or dabbling her black-tipped bill in the surrounding mud. When she gets off to stretch or feed, the tropical sun keeps the egg warm. Small spiral shellfish are the favorite food of flamingos. To feed her baby, the mother first digests the food and then drips the broth from her bill into its mouth. As the young flamingo grows, its straight bill becomes

24

crooked. The upper part of the bill shuts like a lid on the boxlike lower part. Arching its long neck downward until the head is upside down and the bill pointing backward, the flamingo stirs up the mud with its large webbed feet and collects its food. Because the bill is fitted with fine strainers along its edges, the mud washes out and the food stays in. Newly hatched flamingos are covered with white down; the first feathers are grayish white, except on the wings, where they are darker. With each moult the plumage gets pinker, growing more and more rosy until, after several years, it may be scarlet. More often the grown birds have dull pink bodies, and scarlet wings edged with coal-black quills. A standing bird may be about five feet in height. At one time there were flamingo cities along the coast of the southern Atlantic states, but now the birds nest in this country only when they are cared for by humans.

NESTING AREA: Yucatán Peninsula, from the Bahamas south to the coast of Venezuela.

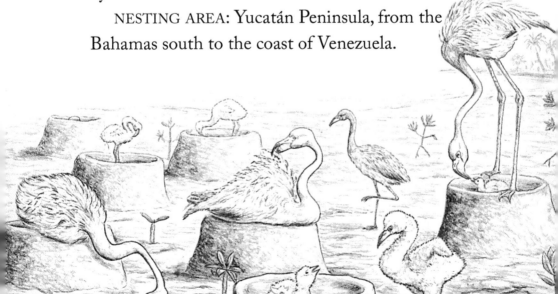

The MEADOWLARK often makes an arch of grass over her nest in order to conceal it, for she is one of the many birds that like some kind of roof over their homes. In a pasture or field she chooses a spot on the ground sheltered by a tuft of grass or clump of weeds. In order to keep the spot completely hidden, the birds use a winding tunnel through the grass as an approach to the side entrance of the nest, which is made up of stems and coarse grass and is lined with fine grass. Two to seven white eggs are laid; they are speckled, more or less thickly, with reddish-brown and lilac spots. The male bird helps the female hatch the eggs and care for the young birds. Two families a year are often raised. Before they learn to fly, the baby birds learn to walk through the runways surrounding the nest. Meadow-larks have long, strong legs and large feet. They spend much of their time walking, but they never run or hop. Their long, pointed bills are well adapted for poking in the ground to find weed seeds and harmful insects. Grasshoppers, caterpillars, and beetles are their favorite food. Meadowlarks are ten to eleven inches in length. The female is smaller than the male. Streaked brown above, the birds have a large black crescent on their bright yellow breasts; the yellow shades to white on the sides and to buff below. The sides are streaked with black, and the head is striped black and pale buff. The white outer edges of the pointed tail feathers are conspicuous when the birds fly. The flight is an alternate fluttering and sailing. Meadowlarks are famous for their song. Sitting on a fence post, the male bird sings endlessly, with a cheerful, varied whistle. The Western variety has a richer, more warbling song. Its coloring is similar to that of the Eastern bird, though somewhat paler. Meadowlarks are not true larks; they belong to the same family as the blackbird.

NESTING AREA: the Eastern variety nests in the Eastern states, down through eastern Mexico, Central America, northern South America, Cuba, and in Canada above the Great Lakes. Look for the Western variety throughout the West and Midwest, and western Canada.

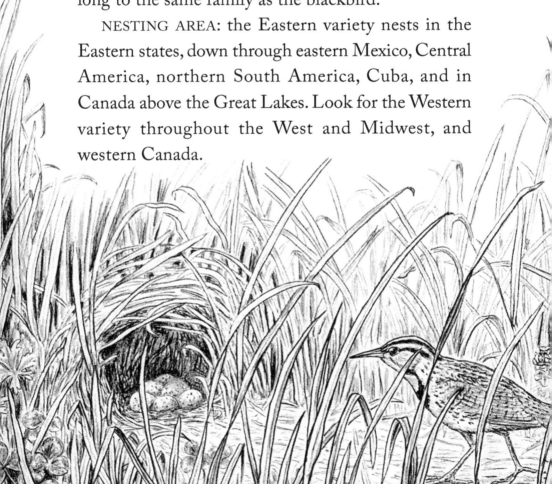

The covered nest of the OVENBIRD is hidden in the woods. These birds choose a secluded spot on the ground among dry leaves, shielded by new spring growth. Usually somewhat sunken, the domed nest is shaped like an old-fashioned oven. The round opening on the side is about three inches wide. The nest, firmly woven of grass, bark strips, and dried leaves, is lined with hairlike roots, fine grass, and similar material. The white eggs, which vary in number from three to six, have reddish-brown spots and speckles. The nest blends so well with its surroundings that it is not easily found unless the scared mother's actions reveal it. When frightened, she tries to distract attention by fluttering away, pretending to be injured. Her tail drops and she chirps piteously, as though badly hurt. Normally, these birds are easily recognized by their characteristic walk. On pink feet, they daintily tread their way over the littered ground or along a fallen log. The scientific name of the ovenbird means "to wave a tail." With flirting tails and bobbing heads, they walk among the dead leaves, their large eyes looking for the grubs and insects that are thir food. Ovenbirds are about six inches long. Above, they are olive green; below, white with broken streaks of black. On the head is a dull orange patch edged with black. The young birds stay with their parents and beg for food until they are fully grown. The Ovenbird's usual song, louder with each repetition, sounds as though they were calling "Teacher! Teacher! Teacher!" Their nickname is teacher bird. It also has a rapid, musical song. Because they slightly resemble a thrush, the Ovenbird is sometimes called the Golden-crowned Thrush; actually they belong to the American Warbler family.

NESTING AREA: Northeastern states, west to the Rockies, and up to northeastern British Columbia.

BLACK-BILLED MAGPIES build a very safe, covered nursery for their young. The actual nest is a bowl of mud lined with grass; all around it and arching over it, large and small sticks are interwoven to form a fortress. The whole mass may be as big as a barrel. On each side of it is a hole leading to the nest. It may be placed sixty feet high in a tall tree, or it may be in a bush. A thorn tree is a favorite site, for its sharp spines give added security. A pair of birds may return each year to the same nest. Magpies are found in sparsely wooded regions. After the nesting season is over, groups of the birds live together, forming noisy flocks. The eggs vary in number and color, but six or seven is the usual number, and they are greenish or grayish, heavily marked with brown and purple

blotches. When the young birds get their feathers they are similar to their parents, though their plumage is duller. The adults are glossy black and white. The black in the wings has a metallic blue sheen, and as the light strikes the tail feathers, they appear to be iridescent green and purple. The tail is very long—about half the entire length of the bird, which is twenty inches from the tip of the black bill to the end of the tail. Magpies eats green leaves, fruit, and berries, but their main food consists of crickets, grasshoppers and other insects, crawfish, and mice. They belong to the same family as the jay and the crow, and share with them the bad habit of robbing the nests of smaller birds.

NESTING AREA: Western states, diagonally north-west into Canada and Alaska.

The little VERDIN builds a large nest. It is like a roughly shaped ball and has a tiny entrance on the side. The nest, perhaps eight inches across, is made of weed stalks and thorny twigs woven together, with spines sticking out in all directions. It is usually placed in a prickly shrub or small desert tree, near the end of a branch, often without a leaf to hide it. It may be from two to twenty feet above the ground. Inside this secure fortress the verdins put a lining of leaves and grasses and then a layer of feathers, to make a soft bed for their three to six eggs. They are pale bluish or greenish white in color and are speckled with reddish brown, chiefly at the large end. The baby birds are fed on inchworms and other soft insects. Verdins often hang upside down while scouting the undersides of leaves for insects to capture. Berries are also eaten. When they get their feathers, the young birds are brownish gray above and lighter below. Until they are adult they do not have the yellow head, nor do they have the chestnut shoulder patches. The female's plumage is similar to the male's but duller. After the nest has been used as a nursery, it is kept in repair and used as a cold-weather shelter. Extra smaller nests are built by individual birds to be used as winter sleeping places. Verdins seem to be able to live without water, for they spend their entire lives in dry desert regions, never leaving their home area. The verdin, whose actions resemble those of a cousin, the chickadee, is about four inches long. For their song, verdins have a series of whistles which can be heard for a long distance. They also have a chattering alarm note.

NESTING AREA: Southwestern states and down into Mexico.

The SOCIAL WEAVER birds of South Africa build a hanging "apartment house" of dry grass for the protection of their nests. For their cooperative building, they choose one of the large thorny acacia trees that grow on the plains, and in its branches they hang innumerable long strands of tough grass. They weave the fibers to form an umbrella-like roof, under which each pair of birds builds a feather-lined nest for two to four speckled brownish eggs. There may be three hundred nests under one roof. After the young birds are reared, the families use the thatched shelter as a shield from wind and rain. Each season the birds build fresh nests below those used previously. As a result, the community house grows larger and larger, until it may at last measure twenty-five feet in width and over five feet in height. The weight of such a mass of grass may break some of the supporting branches and cause part of the house to collapse. The weaver birds are forced to build a new home when the weight is great enough to break the tree trunk, as sometimes happens. Social Weaver birds resemble their close relations, the House Sparrows. They have similar dull coloring, but are smaller. They feed in large flocks and live chiefly on seeds.

NESTING AREA: Southern Africa.

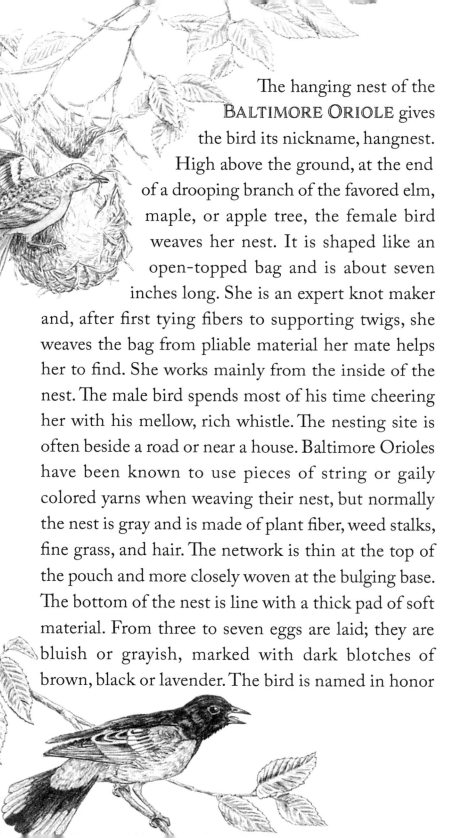

The hanging nest of the BALTIMORE ORIOLE gives the bird its nickname, hangnest. High above the ground, at the end of a drooping branch of the favored elm, maple, or apple tree, the female bird weaves her nest. It is shaped like an open-topped bag and is about seven inches long. She is an expert knot maker and, after first tying fibers to supporting twigs, she weaves the bag from pliable material her mate helps her to find. She works mainly from the inside of the nest. The male bird spends most of his time cheering her with his mellow, rich whistle. The nesting site is often beside a road or near a house. Baltimore Orioles have been known to use pieces of string or gaily colored yarns when weaving their nest, but normally the nest is gray and is made of plant fiber, weed stalks, fine grass, and hair. The network is thin at the top of the pouch and more closely woven at the bulging base. The bottom of the nest is line with a thick pad of soft material. From three to seven eggs are laid; they are bluish or grayish, marked with dark blotches of brown, black or lavender. The bird is named in honor of the founder of Maryland, Lord Baltimore, whose colors were black and yellow. The grown male Oriole has a black head, throat, and upper back. His wings are black with white bars, and there is black in the tail feathers. The rest of the plumage is flame-orange. The females vary, but in general their color is brownish orange above with orange below and in the tail feathers. They become deeper orange with every molt. Young males look similar to adult females; young females are grayish brown with a pale yellow wash. These birds eat caterpillars, other insects, nectar and ripe fruit. They are seven and one half inches long.

NESTING AREA: from the Gulf states northward and into Canada bounded by western Alberta.

The YELLOW PENDULINE TIT builds a hanging nest of plant materials matted together to form a sort of felt. The entrance to the six-inch-long bag is through a tube near the top of the nest. At the entrance there is a hidden, self-closing flap which is sealed by sticky spider webs. The number of eggs laid is uncertain, but nests sheltering two and three young birds have been found. Both females and males are olive-yellow above and bright yellow below, with a light gray stripe running through the eye.

NESTING AREA: equatorial western Africa.

The neatly made, open nest of the RED-EYED VIREO is hung in the horizontal fork of a tree or sapling. There is great variation in the weaving material chosen: fibers of all sorts, plant down, "paper" from wasps' nests, and cobwebs. According to individual taste, the outside of the cup is adorned with lichen, moss, caterpillar and snake skin, bits of paper, cocoons, and other decorative fragments. The inside is lined with grass and other soft material. One to five lightly spotted white eggs are laid. The nestlings are fed on insects and worms collected by their parents from the foliage of trees. The lazy Cowbird often lays her eggs in the nests of the little Vireos. When this happens, the rightful owners may be pushed out by the baby Cowbird, or they may starve because the interloper gulps most of the food. The male Red-eyed Vireo sings his phrases endlessly. He sings when he is hunting food, he sings when taking his turn on the nest, and he just sits and sings. One nickname is preacher. Another is greenlet. *Vireo* means "I am green." Females and males are about five inches long, olive green above and white below. Over the eye, edging the gray cap, is a black-bordered white stripe.

NESTING AREA: lower 48 states except for the Southwest, large portions of Canada.

The OROPENDOLA of tropical South America builds a completely enclosed nest. The male bird does none of the work, nor is he interested in the young birds. The female attaches long plant tendrils to a tree branch and weaves a swaying support for the bag in which she puts the nest, a loose mass of leaves, bark, and fiber. On this mattress she lays two pale-blue eggs, marked with brownish black. She weaves the lower part of the bag, which is about three feet long, from the inside and takes about a month to finish her home. Many birds build in the same tree. The plumage is glossy black and chestnut brown, with yellow feathers in the tail. Oropendolas eat fruit.

NESTING AREA: Central and South America for several different species.

DOWNY WOODPECKERS make a hole in a dead or partly decayed tree for the safe rearing of their four to six baby birds. Their strong, straight, chisel-shaped bills cut the circular entrance. Then the birds hollow out a cavity to the depth of eight to twelve inches, leaving a few chips at the bottom of the hole as a pad for the white eggs. The parents take turns in sitting on the eggs. The male bird has a splash of brilliant red on the back of his head, which distinguishes him from the female. Both birds are black and white above, and white below. When the young birds are feathered, and strong enough to climb from the hole, the parents teach them to hunt for their own food. They eat many kinds of harmful insects and are particularly useful in destroying the grubs that live under the bark of trees. Using their head as a hammer, the woodpecker drives their bill into a tree trunk, making tiny holes. Then they gather up the grub with a very long, barbed tongue. The sound of their tapping is heard in orchards, gardens, and wood lots.

The Downy Woodpecker has stout, rather short legs; the toes are arranged to give great security when climbing a tree. The strong, pointed tail feathers give added support. A little fruit, chiefly wild berries, is included in their diet. Most Downy Woodpeckers spend the winter in their home territory. In the autumn they chisel holes in trees for use in cold weather. The Downy averages six inches in length.

NESTING AREA: continental U.S. with the exception of the arid southwest, the southern half of Canada, and southern portions of Alaska.

BLACK-CAPPED CHICKADEES sometimes nest in a woodpecker's deserted home or, if they cannot find a suitable cavity, make a hole in a rotted tree stump. Moss, grass, and feathers line the bottom of the hole in which the lightly speckled eggs are laid. Nesting time is a busy time for the acrobatic chickadee parents, who may have as many as thirteen baby birds to feed on larvae and insects. Grown birds measure about five inches; they are black, gray, and white.

NESTING AREA: northern half of the lower 48 states, the southern half of Canada and southern portions of Alaska.

For their home, the ELF OWLS make use of the carpenter work of another desert bird. They use a hole made by the Gila Woodpecker. These woodpeckers, finding no suitable wood to peck, make their home in the pithy trunk of the saguaro cactus, a plant which grows to a height of fifty feet. The sap in the cactus, which oozes out as the birds chisel their hole, soon hardens. As a result, the edge of the circular entrance becomes as firm as wood, and the gourd-shaped cavity dries to a hard shell. These holes, high in the cactus, are taken over by the six-inch-long Elf Owls, which use no nesting material. Three is the usual number of oval white eggs laid at the bottom of the eight-inch-deep cavity. The parents take turns in sitting on the eggs, which hatch in just over three weeks. The baby birds are covered with pure white down. Some adult Elf Owls are gray with yellowish spots above, and mixed gray, white, and light brown below; others are more brown than gray. They all have white eyebrows and lemon-yellow eyes. Elf Owls stay in their holes during daylight hours. At night they fly from their shelter in search of such food as grasshoppers, ants, and beetles. Their call is an excited chattering sound. When caught, these midget owls sometimes pretend to be dead: they become limp and do not move.

Then suddenly, they "come to life" and dart away. An Elf Owl may try to hide behind their own wing, stretched across the face. Elf Owls are occasionally found in wooded canyons but are much more frequently seen in the desert.

NESTING AREA: Southwestern states down into Mexico.

HORNBILLS are not found in the Americas. Various kinds of these strange birds are at home in many tropical areas of the Old World. The Great Hornbill, almost five feet long, is the largest member of the family and lives in Southeast Asia, with some still existing in the hilly regions all the way down to Sumatra. At nesting time, the female climbs into a hole, high in a tall tree. Using their bills as trowels, the birds build a wall across the opening, making the nest safe from monkeys, snakes, and other enemies. From the inside, the female, using muck from the bottom of the cavity, does most of the plasterwork. The male helps from the outside. They leave a slit in the hard wall. The female pokes her bill through it, and the male feeds her with fruit and, occasionally, small reptiles and mice. The floor of the cavity is covered with bark fragments, feathers, and decayed material, and on this trash the mother bird lays her rough-surfaced eggs—usually four of them. White at first, they soon become stained dark brown. Not until the young birds are fully feathered is the wall broken away and the imprisoned family freed. Great Hornbills have black feathers on the body, white on the neck and wings; the white tail has a black bar across it. The huge saw-toothed bill is yellow, and the helmet shades

from orange to red. The front and back of the male's helmet are black. His eyes are red; the females are pearly white. A pair of Great Hornbills often uses the same nest hole year after year.

NESTING AREA: Southeast Asia.

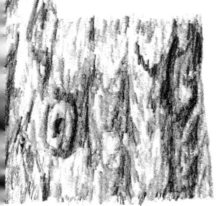

The Burrowing Owl lives in a hole in the ground. Sometimes, if the ground is soft enough, they dig their own holes, but the Western variety of Burrowing Owl usually takes over the home of a prairie dog or some other small animal. Several pairs of owls, each in its own hole, may live close to each other. The nest is from five to ten feet from the mouth of the burrow. About five inches wide at its entrance, the curved passage is enlarged to form a nursery for the young birds, which hatch from pure white eggs. Grass, feathers, livestock manure, and any other available material are used to line the nest. The parents take turns in hatching the eggs. The young birds, from two to twelve in number, are covered with white down when they first break from their shells. Until they are well feathered and able to fly, the owlets stay quite close to the sheltering safety of the burrow. Their first plumage is mostly plain, light grayish brown. The

parent birds are brown with whitish spots above and are paler and barred with brown below. Burrowing Owls are about nine inches in length; they have small round heads, short tails, and long legs. Ordinarily, members of the owl family are active only at night, but these birds of the open prairies are able to see well in broad daylight. During the day, however, they take only short flights and stay near the ground. Burrowing Owls spend much of their time sitting on fence posts or on the branches of low trees or bushes, where they bob and bow in a friendly way. If alarmed, they rush quickly to their burrows, which are used as year-round homes. They call "Cack! Cack!" as they dart to safety. They also make chattering and cooing sounds. Seizing their prey with their claws, these owls eat anything they can catch—from snakes to grasshoppers.

NESTING AREA: many subspecies of Burrowing Owls are found in the Western states, down into Mexico, Florida, the Caribbean and South America.

A hole in the sand or gravel bank beside water is the springtime home of a pair of BELTED KINGFISHERS. They dig the hole themselves, using their long, stout bills as pickaxes and their feet as shovels. The feet are very small but are well fitted for digging. The outer toe of each foot is joined to the middle toe, forming a flat, rough-surfaced sole. Four feet or more from the entrance, the hole, which slopes gradually upward, ends in a widened nest area. Often no nesting material is used, though sometimes the five to eight glossy eggs are laid on a little grass or a few fishbones. When the young birds get feathers, they have the same coloring as their mother. She is white below and blue-gray above and has a blue-gray belt with a reddish band below it. The male has no reddish band. Grown kingfishers are about twelve inches long. When these keen-sighted birds plunge after fish, their oily plumage does not get wet. The young birds rush the burrow's entrance when they hear the rattling cry with which their parents announce dinner.

NESTING AREA: lower 48 states except the Southwest, most of Canada and Alaska.

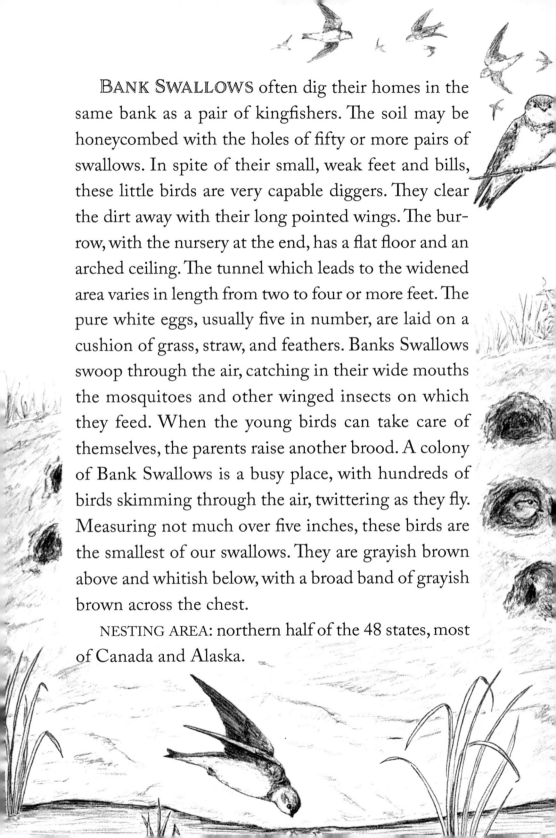

BANK SWALLOWS often dig their homes in the same bank as a pair of kingfishers. The soil may be honeycombed with the holes of fifty or more pairs of swallows. In spite of their small, weak feet and bills, these little birds are very capable diggers. They clear the dirt away with their long pointed wings. The burrow, with the nursery at the end, has a flat floor and an arched ceiling. The tunnel which leads to the widened area varies in length from two to four or more feet. The pure white eggs, usually five in number, are laid on a cushion of grass, straw, and feathers. Banks Swallows swoop through the air, catching in their wide mouths the mosquitoes and other winged insects on which they feed. When the young birds can take care of themselves, the parents raise another brood. A colony of Bank Swallows is a busy place, with hundreds of birds skimming through the air, twittering as they fly. Measuring not much over five inches, these birds are the smallest of our swallows. They are grayish brown above and whitish below, with a broad band of grayish brown across the chest.

NESTING AREA: northern half of the 48 states, most of Canada and Alaska.

CLIFF or EAVE SWALLOWS are birds that have adapted their ways to humans. In remote places they use a cliff for a nesting site, but groups of these swallows frequently choose the eaves of farm buildings. They select a weathered surface, since their mud home will not stick to smooth, painted wood. They collect mud, mixed sometimes with a little straw and hair, and form it into pellets in their mouths. Then they press it into place, smoothing the inner side with the tops of their bills. After the female has outlined the back of the nest with dabs of mud, both birds go to work. First they build a sort of half cup, jutting from the wall. Then, pellet by pellet, they build the back of the wall, the sides, and the roof. The entrance is built out and gives the nest a bottle-like shape. When at last the plasterwork is done, the female adds a thin lining of feathers and other soft material. Three to five eggs are laid; they are white with reddish-brown markings. The nestlings are fed on soft-bodied flying insects, which the parents catch in their short, wide bills. Cliff Swallows are about six inches long; they are steel blue above, with a conspicuous patch of whitish feathers on the forehead and a buff patch near the tail. Below they are red-brown and whitish.

NESTING AREA: most states, north into Canada and Alaska, south into much of Mexico.

BARN SWALLOWS seem to prefer the protection of buildings, though sometimes they nest in caves or on sheltered ledges. They choose the inside of a hayloft or other farm outbuilding, plastering their bowl-shaped nest to a high beam. Built of mud pellets strengthened with straw, it is so thickly lined with feathers from a nearby chicken yard that the padding hangs over the side of the nest. The nest is used to raise two broods a season, and a pair of birds may come back to the same nest the following year. Three to six young are hatched from spotted white eggs. They are fed on winged insects caught by the parents as they fly or swoop low around the farm buildings. The birds twitter a musical song. Barn Swallows, about seven inches long, are shining steel blue above and varying shades of red below. The forked tail has very long outer feathers.

NESTING AREA: North America, Europe, Asia, and North Africa, migrating to all continents except Antarctica.

The WOOD STORK is the only member of the stork family found in the United States.

NESTING AREA: North Carolina to Florida.

The WHITE STORKS of the Old World are welcomed as a sign of good luck wherever they build their open nest of sticks on a roof or chimney. Repaired year after year, the nests reach an immense size. Many are often found close together. A cushion of grass lines a depression in the top of the nest, and there the white eggs, usually four, are laid. A pair of storks, looking alike with their black and white plumage and their red legs and bills, shares the care of the nest. The male, measuring about three and a half feet, sits on the eggs by day; the female, which is smaller, at night. One bird stands guard over the newly hatched babies while the other forages. The young birds vary in size, because incubation begins when the first egg is laid. The last bird to hatch often dies, for the older ones get more of the predigested food that is dropped in the nest by the parents. As the nestlings grow, they help themselves to this food direct from their parents' bills. Later, they are given freshly caught food. Frogs are a favorite of storks, but they eat anything they can catch. They talk to each other by clapping their bills.

NESTING AREA: Europe, North Africa, Southwest Asia.

When CHIMNEY SWIFTS are on migration, countless hundreds of them sleep in a favorite chimney. In the spring the flock breaks up, and each pair selects a chimney of its own for a nesting site. In places where such a shelter is not available, they use a hollow tree, as their ancestors did before convenient chimneys existed. While flying, the birds break short twigs from trees. They glue these to the inside of the chimney to form a flat, rough, basketlike nest. The "glue" is saliva which hardens when exposed to the air. It comes from enlarged glands in the swift's mouth, and the glands shrink at the end of the nesting season. Three to five white eggs are laid. The growing nestlings, heads pointed upward, cling near the nest until they are strong enough to fly. Chimney Swifts' sharp-clawed feet are not built for perching, but they can attach themselves securely to an upright surface with the help of short, stiff tail feathers, which are tipped with needle-like spines. These birds spend all day in the air, twittering joyfully or with their wide mouths open to collect insects. About five and one half inches long, they are dark gray-brown above and paler below.

NESTING AREA: Eastern and Central states, northward into Canada.

The EDIBLE-NEST SWIFTLET of Southeast Asia is also called the White-nest Swiftlet. Soup made from their nests is considered a delicacy in China. Made entirely of the birds' saliva, the nests are like jelly when softened in water. Some nests contain bits of moss, straw, or other material, which is removed by hand before making the soup. In the 1990s, people began building rooftop bird houses in Southeast Asia to harvest nests up to four times a year, allowing time for the chicks to fledge. The nests are often called the "Caviar of the East" and cost thousands of dollars per kilogram. These birds are similar in many ways to Chimney Swifts, but they do not have spine-tail feathers. Edible-nest Swiftlets are brown above and white below. Two is the usual number of eggs laid; they are white. Large colonies of up to a million swiftlets glue their nests to the rocky walls of caves near the sea.

NESTING AREA: Southeast Asia.

The EASTERN WHIP-POOR-WILL makes no nest at all. When other birds are busy collecting material and building their nests, the Eastern Whip-poor-will just looks for a carpet of leaves in the deep woods. Often she selects a secluded spot beside a bush. There she lays two eggs. Marked with spots, the eggs blend perfectly with the dry leaves. The bird's plumage is also mixed in color, which makes her almost impossible to see when she is sitting on the eggs. She seems to know this and generally sits motionless when an intruder comes near. But, like many other ground-nesting birds, if she is frightened away from her home she has the trick of acting as though badly injured. When she thinks that her eggs are safe from discovery, she recovers and flies noiselessly away. Sometimes she seems to decide that the chosen place is no longer a satisfactory hideaway; then she moves the eggs. Nobody knows how she carries them—perhaps she picks them up in her large mouth. When the down-covered baby birds hatch, they are invisible among the twigs and dead leaves. Sometimes the mother bird spirits them away, too, like the eggs. The Eastern Whip-poor-will has a short but extremely wide bill fringed with stiff bristles. The first part of its scientific name means "cave mouth." At night the birds fly zigzag through the woods with their mouths wide open to trap fat moths and other winged insects. Once inside the "cave," the insects' escape is prevented by the bristles. In the daylight the birds spend much of their time crouched on the ground. If they sit on a branch they do not perch across it, because of their small feet; they squat lengthwise. The male and female birds have similar mixed gray, black, brown, and buff plumage with a white band across the throat. The three outer tail feathers of the male are partly white. The call of the whip-poor-will gives him his name. At dusk and at night he repeats "Whip-poor-will!" over and over and over again. The second part of its scientific name, *vociferous,* means "strong voice." In between calls, he says "Chuck!" very quietly.

NESTING AREA: Eastern states. Whip-poor-wills were split into two species in 2010 based on mitochondrial DNA. The Mexican Whip-poor-will nests in the Western states down into Mexico.

The KILLDEER, a member of the plover family, makes no nest. A bare depression in the ground is the usual nest, though sometimes the birds put a few bits of wood, weed stalks, or pebbles in or around the hollow. A favorite placed for a killdeer nursery is an open field, where the thickly spotted and blotched eggs blend with the color of the ground. The eggs are neatly arranged with the pointed ends all toward the center. Four baby birds make up the usual killdeer family. They are not helpless when hatched. As soon as they are dry they run around and feed themselves, though their parents help them find grubs and bugs. The adult birds fly fast but, because their flight feathers grow slowly, the young birds are unable to fly until they are almost fully grown. They rely for safety on the protective coloration of their gray, rusty brown, and white plumage, which acts as a camouflage. The parents take good care of the eggs

and the baby birds. If trouble seems near, the mother bird tries to lure the predator away by pretending she is hurt. She screams and acts as though her wings were broken, flopping along and feigning exhaustion. The male bird acts as a sentinel. He circles overhead, making all the noise he can and calling "Killdee! Killdee!" This call gives the bird its name; in some places they are known as Killdee instead of Killdeer. Since they eat enormous numbers and varieties of insect pests, Killdeers are very valuable birds. After the nesting season they collect in groups, and flocks of them haunt the seashore and other areas near water. They are olive brown above and white below and are banded with black on the head and breast. Adult birds have two bands across the breast; young birds, one. Two families are often reared in a season.

NESTING AREA: lower 48 states, most of Canada, the northern half of Mexico and portions of the west coast of South America.

The SAGE GROUSE scratches a slight hollow in the ground under a sage bush, and her nest is made. She lays seven to nine greenish or greenish-yellow eggs, marked with round, dark spots. The Sage Grouse matches the color of the ground and is difficult to see when she is sitting motionless on her nest. The male bird does not help with the incubating or with the care of the young chicks, which are ready to run from the nest the first fifteen minutes after they leave the egg. They are fluffy and their color is a mottled yellow-brown. In the autumn, when the young birds are fully grown, many families join together in groups. Formerly, thousands of these birds could be see awaiting their turn to drink at a spring or water hole, but now they are becoming scarce. In the early spring, the males perform a peculiar dance. At dawn a number of them appear on their parade ground and strut, with their pointed tail feathers raised and spread, their wings drooped, and bare patches of skin on their necks inflated like balloons. Stiff white feathers, surrounding these air sacs, stick out in all directions. The display is accompanied by croakings and rasping noises, and when the air is expelled from the sacs it makes a rumbling sound. The male Sage Grouse is as large as a small turkey and may be thirty inches in length. The females are smaller and have shorter tails. The plumage of both sexes is variegated black, brown, and yellowish above, and yellow-white below, but the female has no neck decorations. The Sage Grouses' legs and feet are feathered to the toes. Their main food is sagebrush leaves, but they—particularly the young birds—also eat insects.

NESTING AREA: sagebrush country of western North America.

The male OSTRICH is the nest maker of the family. He scratches a hollow in the sand and persuades two, three, or more females to lay their eggs in it. There may be twenty or more creamy yellow eggs, each weighing three to four pounds, in the nest. The females usually leave most of the incubating to the male. He sits on the nest all night. In cool areas, a female relieves him for short periods during the day so that he can get some food. In hot regions, the eggs are covered with sand and kept warm by the sun while the male is away. Ostriches eat reptiles, insects, small mammals, and birds, as well as fruit, seeds, and leaves. They swallow small stones to help digest their food. The baby ostriches, which have stiff little feathers, can take care of themselves soon after they are out of the eggs, but the male bird watches over them. The young

birds are mottled brown, yellow, and white. The adult males, sometimes eight feet tall, are black, with pure white tail feathers and wing plumes. The females are smaller and are brownish gray. The necks of ostriches are covered with short down; the powerful legs are bare. Their feet, which have only two toes, have fleshy pads on the underside. Although ostriches cannot fly, they use their short, fluffy-feathered wings to help them run. They can sprint very fast—at 43 miles per hour. When ostrich plumes were the fashion, great numbers of these birds were kept in captivity for the sake of the plumes, which were cut regularly. Today there are still ostrich farms, since there is demand for the meat and feathers, and the leatherlike skin is also valued.

NESTING AREA: dry, open plains of Africa.

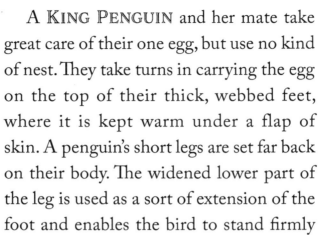

A KING PENGUIN and her mate take great care of their one egg, but use no kind of nest. They take turns in carrying the egg on the top of their thick, webbed feet, where it is kept warm under a flap of skin. A penguin's short legs are set far back on their body. The widened lower part of the leg is used as a sort of extension of the foot and enables the bird to stand firmly erect. The penguin's posture is upright when she walks. She can shuffle along with the egg or the newly hatched, downy chick on her insteps. Thousands of these trumpeting birds live together in colonies. They are comfortable in a cold climate, because they are kept warm by a layer of fat under the skin. King penguins are three feet tall. They are bluish gray, with glistening white breasts which shade to orange at the throat. Their black heads have yellow markings on the sides. Penguins cannot fly, but they make good use of their flipper-like wings when they dive and swim. The wings act as oars and the feet as a rudder when penguins are searching the sea for fish that is their food.

NESTING AREA: islands near the Antarctic.